Printed in the United States of America

First Edition, 2016

ISBN: 978-1-48358-335-8

D0558443

Dedication

This book is dedicated to my daughters, Hannah and Amy, who were good sports about traveling around the world with us. I look forward to many more adventures with you!

Fast Facts About

CONTINENT
South America

POPULATION
30,444,999

CAPITAL CITY
Lima

LANGUAGES
Spanish, Quechua (keh-choo-ah), Aymara

CURRENCY
Nuevos (noo-eh-bohs) Soles (soh-lays)

Table of Contents

Introduction

HELLO
my name is

Hannah

HELLO
my name is

Amy

Hi! My name is Hannah. And my name is Amy. In September, 2015, our parents took us on a Round the World trip for 6 months! We know that most kids don't get to travel around the world, so our Mom made these books as a way for you to come along the adventure with us.

Since we are girls and we like to learn, we are inspired by Let Girls Learn, a U.S. government initiative to improve access to education for girls around the world. For every book sold we are going to make a $1 donation to support projects that increase access to a quality education for girls.

Happy travels!

P.S. If your parents want to know what it's like to travel around the world with kids, our parents wrote about it on the Nature Adventurers blog at:

natureadventurersblog.com.

Traveling Around the World

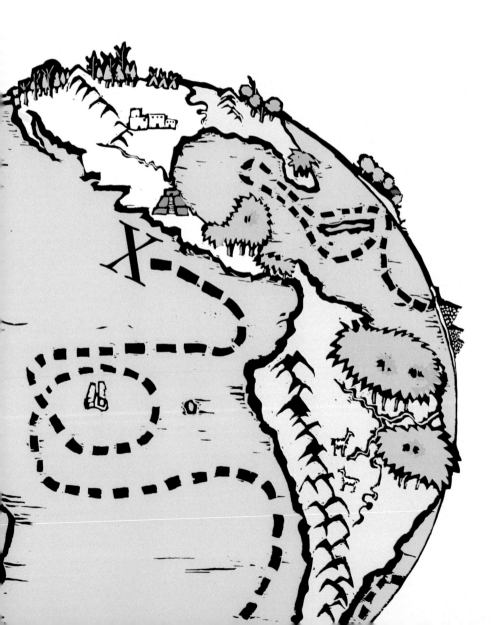

From September, 2015, to March, 2016, we got to travel around the world with our parents!

That meant we didn't have to go to school. YAY!

Though we still had to do 'school work' while we traveled through 5 continents and 10 countries. BOO!

From North America to South America

Our first stop was Peru. Peru is in South America. To get there, we had to fly from San Francisco to Los Angeles and change planes just after midnight. Then we flew on to Lima, the capital city of Peru.

In Los Angeles, we were so tired, and it took forever to change planes. We had to wait on a bus for a long time, then it drove us to the next airplane. We were glad we had our stuffed animals to snuggle with while we waited.

Visiting the Capital

Lima is a city of over 10 million people! It was big and noisy. The cars beeped their horns a lot. Sometimes it was to see if we wanted a taxi.

There were a lot of fun things to do in Lima. We went to an indoor play factory, made chocolate (yum, yum), discovered an outdoor piano and got our wiggles out at a playground.

Huaca Pucllana

Our Mom and Dad also took us to Huaca (ooh-ah-kah) Pucllana. The Lima people (an indigenous civilization) used to live here between 200 AD and 700 AD.

The Lima used clay bricks to make their adobe and pyramid, and placed the bricks vertically instead of horizontally, so the buildings would not collapse in an earthquake (cool, hey!).

We also learned that the Lima ate guinea pig. Some modern-day Peruvians still eat it. Eew, not us though! We liked eating a cinnamon roll at the cafe!

Cusco

After a couple of days in Lima, we flew to Cusco (Cuzco) in the Urubamba Valley (Sacred Valley). At 3,399 m (11,152 ft) above sea level, Cusco is one of the highest elevated cities in the world!

We visited the museums and catacombs of the San Francisco Convent in Cusco (Museo y Catacumbas del Convento de San Francisco de Cusco is how you say it in Spanish). Though we were more interested in the cats that lived there and the ice cream we had just outside the Convent!

Sillacancha

From Cusco, we drove to a tiny town in the Sacred Valley named Sillacancha (See-ya-kan-chah). We stayed there for nine nights.

We loved our house in Sillacancha because it had a swing chair, four beds for us to choose between, and wild mint to make tea with.

It even had a firepit for roasting marshmallows (yum, yum!). It was super hard to find marshmallows in Peru, but after looking through many stores, we finally found some (even if they were fruity flavored)!

Can you believe we had no TV in Sillacancha...just the Andean mountains to look at?! We passed the time by playing games such as Go Fish, doing our homework (aren't our parents so mean for making us do homework on a trip?), and exploring the surrounding area.

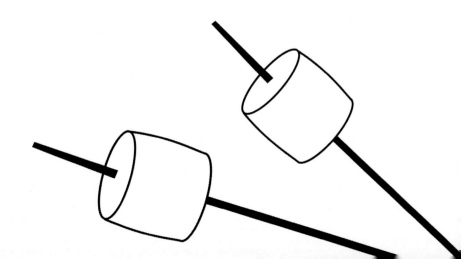

Exploring the Ruins of the Sacred Valley

We visited ancient ruins in Pisac, Moray, and Machu Picchu (a famous site of the Inca civilization). We had to do a lot of walking, and sometimes it was too much, especially for Amy's 5 year old legs (she hadn't turned 6 yet)!

We also had to get up super early, then wait in a long line for the bus to Machu Picchu. We were cranky at first, but felt better after having ice cream and coming across the llamas and alpacas in Machu Picchu.

Exploring Other Sites in the Sacred Valley

We also went to a salt mine, a Peruvian market, and a textile center where we learned how wool is cleaned, dyed and woven into beautiful products.

We loved walking through the salt mines, seeing all the Peruvian crafts in the market, and picking out some knitted finger puppets at the textile center. Hannah also went to the Urubamba market with our Dad, which she liked.

Our favorite part was learning that red dye is made from squishing a parasite that is found on cactus. When we got back to the house, we tried it for ourselves and got dye all over our hands. It was so much fun getting messy!

People of Peru

The people of Peru primarily speak Spanish, though some of our tour guides spoke Quechua (the main language of the Incas, and still spoken in Peru today).

Even though we only speak a little bit of Spanish, we were able to communicate with each other okay.

Most of the people in the cities dress like we do, however; the people who live in rural areas, such as the Andes mountains, have a more traditional way of dressing.

We noticed that the women wore their hair in long braids. We hope our hair is that long some day!

The people were very kind and helpful, particularly when we were taking local buses.

Animals of Peru

Our favorite part was meeting the animals of Peru. These included the llamas, alpacas, vicuña's (bee-coo-gnah) and the Andean condor at the animal rescue center (Santuario Animal de Ccochahuasi).

That's where we bought our stuffed llama and alpaca. Hannah named hers Blacky.

Amy named hers Fluffy.

Other Animals in Peru

We also passed a lot of donkeys, sheep, cows and goats along the road.

Can you believe that sometimes we had to wait for the donkeys and sheep to cross the road before we could continue driving? That was crazy!

Although you can find these animals everywhere, we can't forget to mention all the dogs (stray and otherwise) we met in Peru.

We love dogs!

Back to Lima

After our time in the Sacred Valley, we flew back to Lima for two more days.

This time we visited the zoo, where many Peruvian school children kept asking my Dad to say their name in English! It was so funny!

We saw giant tortoises from the Galápagos Islands, beautiful peacocks, a hippopotamus pooping in it's water hole, and the red bum of the Baboons!

We'd eventually get to see all of these animals in the wild on our trip, except the tortoises.

Adios, Peru

While we only saw a small part of Peru, we hope you enjoyed exploring it with us!

Please join us on our next adventure as we travel to Brazil!

Adiós! Hasta luego!

Glossary

Alpaca - a domesticated animal (an animal not found in the wild) found in the high Andes mountain range in South America. Alpacas are used for their wool.

Catacombs - an underground place where people are buried.

Indigenous people - a group of people who were living naturally in a particular region or environment.

Llama - a South American animal, with a long neck, that lives in the Andes. Llamas are used to carry things, and for their wool.

Parasite - an organism that lives in or on another organism and gets food or protection from it.

Quechua - a family of languages spoken by the Indian people of Peru, Bolivia, Ecuador, Chile and Argentina.

Sacred Valley (of the Incas) - also known as Urubamba Valley, in the Andes of Peru, close to the Inca capital of Cusco and the ancient city of Machu Picchu.

Vicuña - a large South American animal, related to the llama and alpaca. Its wool is used to make clothing.

Thank You!

Thank you for traveling to Peru with us. For more information about our Round the World trip, please visit: natureadventurersblog.com

We hoped you enjoyed reading the book as much as our Mom enjoyed writing it. Let us know what you thought about the book by leaving a review on Amazon, or leaving a comment on the Nature Adventurers blog (with the help of your parents, of course!) This will help our Mom write even better books about the other countries we visited.

Hannah **and** Amy

I would also like to thank my editor, Susan Kiley, who did an amazing job helping me bring this book to life, as well as Ana Galán, who provided the Spanish pronunciation guide. Thanks also to Ari Gold and his team, who designed the beautiful cover and layout for the book. Pat Flynn's 'eBooks the Smart Way' and Chandler Bolt's 'Book Launch' were invaluable in guiding me through this process. Last, but not least, I would like to thank my husband, co-parent, and traveling partner, Anthony Rizk for being daring enough to travel around the world with our family!

Sabrina Rizk

natureadventurersblog.com